Public Art Project Management Handbook –by John Weeden
Table of Contents:

Abstract:

1. Project Development

This section will address the various factors that affect the decision of whether to cultivate a specific project or to follow other possibilities. Variables covered include site selection issues, budget projections, and suitable art types and materials. Furthermore, techniques for cultivating substantive participation from community groups will be described in detail, as shall methods for building sustainable relationships with governmental authorities whose support is necessary for the successful realization of the project. As a final layer to this section, attention will be directed toward the composition of RFQ's and RFP's, the differences between the two, and the rationales for using one over the other depending on the circumstance.

Section Topics:
Site Selection
Budget Projections
Government Engagement
RFQ/RFP Composition
Community Engagement

2. Committees and Coordination

A project's success is defined by more than the completion of the project on time and within budget. In the public art world, 'success' also depends on the degree to which it has fostered a sense of ownership on the part of those that participated in its production. Committees are instrumental in cultivating pride in the finished product and the process by which it came to be. When its dynamics are appropriately aligned, a group of committed and informed individuals representing all project stakeholders can make something truly remarkable happen for its community. This section will describe methods of composing committees that are capable of guiding great art projects to completion, as well as act as effective ambassadors for the public art program's value to the community overall.

Section Topics:
Composition Dynamics
Expertise and Influence
Roles and Expectations
Coordination
Community Engagement

3. Artist Selection

Methods of artist selection for public art projects vary depending on the size of the budget, the profile of the project, and the complexity of the type of work desired. It is also the most crucial aspect of the entire endeavor. If the 'right' artist is chosen virtually any obstacle can be overcome. Conversely, if the 'wrong' artist is selected for the project, almost nothing will go as planned. In this chapter techniques for thoroughly coordinating the artist selection phase of your public art program will be detailed.

2

4. Project Management

Projects come to fruition because of the effective coordination of various elements in a professional fashion by your organization's staff. Balancing the demands, schedules, and different working cultures of artists, vendors, government officials, and the general public is both a science and an art. Keeping all stakeholders engaged, committed, and in step throughout the process requires strategic planning and discernment. This section will engage specific processes for guiding the myriad considerations of any project into a coherent and cohesive conclusion that your community can claim with pride.

5. Inventory and Maintenance

As a city's public art collection grows, it is imperative that its art works be maintained in a manner appropriate to the materials and installation setting of each piece. A major consideration is how routine conservation and major repairs are funded once a project's primary budget is fully spent. This section will cover issues to do with record keeping for completed projects, appropriate conservation methods, and financing options for ensuring budgets for maintenance are sustainable.

Section 1: Project Development

This section will address the various factors that affect the decision of whether to cultivate a specific project or to follow other possibilities. Variables covered include site selection issues, budget projections, and suitable art types and materials. Furthermore, techniques for cultivating substantive participation from community groups will be described in detail, as shall methods for building sustainable relationships with governmental authorities whose support is necessary for the successful realization of the project. As a final layer to this section, attention will be directed toward the composition of RFQ's and RFP's, the differences between the two, and the rationales for using one over the other depending on the circumstance.

Section Topics:
Site Selection
Budget Projections
Government Engagement
RFQ/RFP Composition
Community Engagement

Site Selection:

If multiple sites are available, then the Project Manager should scout site prospects and review options with their contacts in the appropriate City administration department, such as Engineering, Public Works, Planning, Land Development, or Real Estate, etc.

Once these possible sites are confirmed as available for developing a project, preferences for what kind of project should be composed. Artwork should be compatible in scale, material, form, and content with its environmental and architectural surroundings. If desired to serve a functional purpose, artworks may establish focal points; modify, enhance or define specific spaces; establish identity or address specific issues of civic design.

Consideration should also be given to the historical, geographical, demographic, and social/cultural context of the site or community, as well as the intended use of the site and way people are most likely to interact with the artwork. Completed artworks should be able to respond to the specific contextual issues of the particular project and its surrounding community.

For example, if an exterior children's playground is targeted for an art installation, variables to include in planning might include: routine maintenance, safety for climbing, structural strength, and durability in the natural elements. An unfortunate possibility to proactively plan against is the chance of vandalism in the form of spray painted graffiti, or even arson. There are a number of clear coatings that can be applied to a variety of surfaces that make cleaning graffiti relatively simple and cost-effective. Arson damage is more serious, but can be mitigated or prevented by commissioning works constructed from non-flammable materials such as steel, stone, or concrete, rather than plastic, wood, or fibers.

If project budgets are earmarked for projects tied to specific sites, these same considerations may still be used for determining the type of artwork installed.

Budget Projections:

When planning project budgets, a number of variables need to be taken into account. If a 'Percent-for-Art' model sets funding, then your budget will be pre-determined. However, if you are attempting to develop outside resources to supplement municipal funding, you will need to have a realistic goal amount to present to prospective partners. In either case, certain guidelines are applicable no matter what the scenario you are facing.

Issues to take into consideration include:

1. Payments Turnaround. What is the overall turn-around time required to process a payment once the artist completes a benchmark and submits an invoice. How many steps are required in order for the invoice to be accepted and their check cut by the appropriate municipal authority? How many people have to sign off on it, from how many different departments at City Hall, etc. Will they accept electronic invoices, or only hard copies? Do they offer electronic direct deposits, or only process via paper check through the US Postal Service? All these factors should be diagrammed in order to understand the general duration of payments so that artists can keep working instead of having to wait without notice of when they can purchase materials, hire contractors, and complete project benchmarks. This aspect is crucial to ensuring a project's timely completion and the satisfaction of artists, stakeholders, and the community alike.

2. Committees: If there is more than one committee that requires voting to approve project benchmarks, the calendar timeframe between committee meetings should be taken into account, as well as the possibility that committees may not approve the actions they are asked to vote on. Committee refusals cause project delays, as benchmarks are pushed back, and payments postponed. In the meantime, contractors may be waiting on payments from artists, and may refuse to continue work until they are paid, complicating matters further.

3. Materials Cost Fluctuation. If committee approval or payments processing takes too long, it is possible for material costs to rise in the interim. Metals are especially subject to such market forces. This can affect the scale of the project originally proposed, unless additional funds can be raised from outside grants or donors.

4. Artwork Type: In general, murals extend the budget further than sculptures simply because paint is less expensive than concrete and steel. They also require less technical expertise in terms of structural engineering and assistance from outside contractors. Furthermore, they are rarely subject to code inspections or ADA compliance regulations (Americans with Disabilities Act), which add to project costs.

Sample Budget Worksheet:

Project: _____   **Total amount of commission: $** _____

General
Artist design fee (Minimum 10% of total budget, maximum 20%)   _____

Professional/Consultant Fee's (Architect, Structural Engineer)   _____

Expenses-applicable only to this project
(Transportation to meeting, copies, postage, phone, fax, etc.)   _____

Insurance (General Liability, Workers' Comp, Automobile)   _____

Documentation
(Photographs, video or other process documentation)   _____

Fabrication
Preparatory Materials (Working Drawings, Model, Templates)   _____

Labor (Assistants, Subcontractors, Fabricators or Artist)   _____

Materials (For fabrication)   _____

Tools/Equipment Rental (If needed for fabrication)   _____

Space rental/Storage (If additional space is needed)   _____

Installation
Delivery of Project/Components   _____

Labor (Subcontractors)   _____

Display Details
(Framing, Footing, Pedestals, Mechanical Devices)   _____

Site Preparation (May be provided in project budget)   _____

Signage (Permanent label identifying artwork)   _____

Other
Contingency (Generally 5-10% of the budget) *Required   _____

Total Project Budget   _____

Because turnaround times for payment processing can be sometimes unpredictable and prolonged, one method of ensuring the project's steady progress is to structure the budget's payment benchmarks in such a way that the artist is provided with enough funds on the front end of the project to get started and keep working while subsequent benchmarks are met and invoices work their way through the system.

Example payment schedule for a $50,000 project:

	Design Payment Schedule - (10% of budget: $5,000)	
A	10% execution of agreement	$500
B	40% schematic design acceptance	$2,000
C	40% final design acceptance	$2,000
D	10% final acceptance (project completion)	$500
	Fabrication Payment Schedule - (90% of budget: $45,000)	
1	45% at begin fabrication	$20,250
2	25% at 50% completion	$11,250
3	25% at fabrication complete	$11,250
4	5% at installation complete	$2,250

Notice that maintenance is not included in the budget breakdown cited above, as such costs should ideally be funded as a separate fund drawn the Percent-for-Art fund. For example, if the total amount of the budget for the Percent-for-Art program in one year amounts to 500,000, then 0.01 percent of that amount should be reserved for ongoing maintenance of the collection of artworks for which the public art agency is responsible, or $5,000. Over time, this fund would grow as each year's allocation is added to the pool. If an artwork gets damaged and requires repairs exceeding the amount available in the pool, additional funds should be sought via grants and private fundraising.

As a general rule, the public art agency should not pay suppliers and fabricators on the artist's behalf from the Artwork Budget, instead of them receiving the funds and making a payment. Such actions can expose the agency to liability issues.

Typically, payments for invoices should be processed as follows:
- The artist turns in an invoice to the public art agency that includes supporting documentation. (Ex. Subcontractor invoices, vendor receipts, etc.)
- The public art agency submits an invoice to the client (municipal or private).
- The client sends payment to the public art agency.
- The public art agency sends payment to the artist.

It should be made clear during the artist's contract signing and orientation, that the public art agency is NOT the funder of the project, but simply the coordinator on behalf of the client (municipal or private). As such, the public art agency must follow the protocols set by the client and must be forwarded funds by them in order to then provide monies to the artist.

Government Engagement:

A vibrant public art program funded by the municipal 'Percent-for-Art' model is reliant on strong relations between the public art agency and the government entities that determine the funding for projects and programs. These relationships are best established and maintained through proactive communication on the part of the public art agency.

Periodical bulletins of upcoming projects, community engagement activities, testimonials about projects' positive impact, and profiles on the artists involved, etc., can easily be formatted into an electronic newsletter for distribution to government officials as well as general supporters, community members, and artists. In such documents photographs tend to hold viewers' attention more than text-heavy blocks.

A specialized document with relevant statistics including local artist participation, community engagement numbers, and budget breakdowns tracking how project funds are allocated should be provided to the appropriate government body in an annual report-style format, replete with photographs of the projects in situ, but also in the process of fabrication, as well as surrounded by community members interacting with the installed artwork. Dedication ceremonies where the community, the artist, their assistants, and government officials are invited are excellent opportunities to celebrate the project's successful completion and to document the impact of the public art agency's work.

These pieces should be considered basic advocacy tools in demonstrating the relevance of public art to building vibrancy, uniqueness, and cohesion within the community at large. When faced with officials or stakeholders that are unfamiliar with the impact or use-value of public art, it is often useful to provide them with some basic terms to make them acquainted with the benefits such projects impart to their surroundings. The sample text below articulates the use-value of public in colloquial terms easy to comprehend. Adapt it, or expand upon it, as it may best suit the needs and circumstances of your own programs.

Public Art's Impact

The arts fuel creativity unlike any other human endeavor. Creativity fosters problem solving, improvisation, teamwork, risk taking and, perhaps most importantly, creativity drives innovation. Without innovation nothing new ever gets done, social ills are never appropriately addressed, businesses go bankrupt, and cities stagnate. The arts are creativity embodied in concrete form. They produce what I've often called 'the what else effect.' Art provokes one to have ideas. When one day there is a vacant lot or a blank wall, and the next there is a sculpture park or mural painting, people's instinctual inclination is (most often) to wonder 'what else' could be done to other blank spaces within the area.

Encounters of art in public spaces causes passersby to wonder what else is possible? With that question of possibility comes an enhanced opportunity to take the next step in the thinking process of how one can actually take part in the shaping of the visual streetscape. When the arts are woven into the landscape of the city its inhabitants are more easily transformed from passive consumers to active contributors of the mettle with which their collective culture is constructed. Which, leads me to my next point...art in public places produces connectivity.

Connectivity means that the denizens of a particular place feel a connection to the area in which they live. Art enables this condition of connectivity in that neighbors often play a crucial role in determining what form their particular mode of arts practice takes within their own neighborhood. Whether it's a mural, or outdoor film series, a sculpture project, or an all weather stage for music, dance and theatre performances, when people take an interest in what happens in their own 'yard,' so to speak, you've suddenly got localized stakeholders with a desire to see something special take place.

Art in public places engenders this sort of 'something special,' most often in the form of common experiences and the concomitant stories shared by all who took part in the making of them. Art of this sort empowers voices to be heard that may not have had an outlet otherwise. It enables people to have a say in how their world works in the most literal and immediate way imaginable: by choosing the way one's world looks. This connectivity phenomenon leads to my final point of community.

When people feel this kind of connection, this pride of ownership built through their own creative output, they tend to want to take care of their community because it matters to them more than something in which they've had neither say nor participation. They want to make sure that the arts comprising the unique social landmarks that signify the character, values, hopes and dreams of that community are respected. The shared stories initiated by the creative experiences of the arts in public places then contribute to the weaving of a more tightly knit community at large; one that cares about its collective future for generations to come, as well as the well being of its individual constituents in the here and now.

To summarize into 'elevator speech' terms...the arts fuel creativity, which drives increased interest to discover new possibilities for the public realm. This creative contribution of the public to the visual landmarks of its neighborhood breeds connectivity to the area through shared story making and telling. Connectivity, in turn, builds stronger, more sustainable communities by giving people something to care about that would not have been accessible otherwise.

~John Weeden

RFQ/RFP Composition:

Projects undertaken by artists or acquisitions of artwork whether by commission, purchase, gift, or other means should further the purpose and goals of the public art program. The public art agency should establish a pool of artists/candidates for each project based on the considerations described below, which should be included in an either a Request for Qualifications (RFQ) or a Request for Proposals (RFP). The primary difference between these two documents is the inclusion of an original sketch or design illustrating an original concept. Such drawings are considered intellectual property in many cases, and should be compensated with a stipend, if requested in the form of an RFP. If the public art agency simply wishes to see an artist's qualifications based on their resume and portfolio of past work, an RFQ without an original proposal should suffice. This warrants no stipend. Many public art organizations will announce their project in the form of an RFQ to elicit an initial large batch of applicants, then select a small number from which to request proposals with designs for which they will provide stipends before making a final decision about whom to commission.

Selection committees should apply the following criteria when selecting artists, considering acquisitions or determining sites for artworks.

Artistic Merit
The inherent quality and excellence of a proposed artwork together with the strength of the artist's concept and design capabilities are the program's highest priorities. Other artistic credentials to consider include training and critical or other professional recognition.

Context
Artwork should be compatible in scale, material, form, and content with its surroundings. When serving a functional purpose, artworks should establish focal points; modify, enhance or define specific spaces; establish identity or address specific issues of civic design. Consideration should also be given to the architectural, historical, geographical, and social/cultural context of the site or community, as well as the way people may interact with the artwork. They must be able to respond to the specific contextual issues and considerations of the particular project, its community and users.

Relevant Experience
Artists should provide convincing evidence of their ability to successfully complete the project as proposed. Particularly on collaborative or design team projects, artists should demonstrate an ability to:
  • Communicate effectively and elicit the ideas of team members;
  • Exhibit flexibility and problem-solving skills;
  • Work with architectural drawings and construction documents;
  • Engage community representatives in a project.
  • Successfully manage all aspects of the project including budgets, committees, sub-contractors, installers and other construction and administrative logistics.

Permanence/Maintenance
Due consideration should be given to the structural and surface soundness, operational costs and inherent resistance to theft, vandalism, weathering and excessive maintenance. Artist should include recommended methods and schedules for maintenance.

Technical Feasibility
An artist must exhibit a successful track record of construction and installation of artwork or show that an appropriate professional has examined the proposed artwork and confirmed feasibility of construction and installation.

Budget
An artist's proposal should provide a budget adequate to cover all costs for the design, fabrication, insurance, transportation, storage, and installation of the proposed artwork, plus reasonable unforeseen circumstances. Artists should have a history of completing projects within budget.

Diversity
Artwork should be sought from artists of diverse racial and cultural identities and from local, regional, national, and international artists.

Fabrication and Installation Schedules
The artist proposal should include a project timeline that incorporates design review, fabrication, delivery and installation in accordance with project schedule. The artist should have a history of completing projects on time.

Selection committees may recommend rejection of all submissions if none are considered satisfactory and a new pool of artists may be established.

ARTIST RESTRICTIONS:

General Restrictions
Artists or members of their immediate families who serve on selection committees, oversight boards, municipal government entities, or the public art agency staff should not be commissioned or receive any direct financial benefit from the public art program during their tenure on either of those bodies.

No artist should receive more than two art enhancement commissions under any five-year period.

Local Artist Participation Requirements
One of the goals of many public art programs is to foster and celebrate the talents of local artists. Requiring a certain percentage of the artwork created with Percent-for-Art funds during any five-year period to be produced by local artists is a common occurrence. Definitions of what constitutes 'local' vary, but general descriptions include a timeframe of residence in the area, and a geographic boundary of a certain radius surrounding the city.

Diversity Goals
In an effort to promote equality and diversity, the public art program should include significant participation by Minorities and Women.

Inappropriate Communication with Selection Committee
The public art agency's staff should be responsible for all correspondence and communication by and between artists applying for percent for art projects and members of selection panels. Discussion by and between any applicant artist and any member of a selection committee outside of regularly scheduled

meetings for such purpose during the selection process should be considered grounds for the disqualification of the artist. Such determination should be made at the sole discretion of the public art agency or its oversight board.

Community Engagement:

A project's success should be measured not only by coming in on time and on budget, but by the extent to which it is embraced by the community in which it exists. Without the active support of the community for the project and the program that produced it, advocacy for future projects grows difficult, and the outlook for future funding becomes precarious. Communication throughout every step of the process is key to building trust with community leaders that will then be best able to coordinate crowds for feedback sessions and design charrettes in the future. Electronic newsletters, and project-specific distribution lists for sending pertinent email updates are excellent tools. However, in some cases where communities are economically stressed or of an older generation, access to current technologies may be limited, so it will be incumbent upon the public art program to contact community members via telephone, hard copy pamphlets through the US Postal Service, or even by visiting local town hall meetings and requesting your item be placed on the agenda.

Community engagement in the form of brainstorming possible subjects for artworks to be set in areas rich in local history is crucial. Likewise, it is advisable to gather the thoughts of the community in order to ascertain the distinct character of the neighborhood, what makes it unique within the larger city and environs. As selection committees are composed, it will be important to recruit members of the actual community in which the piece is to be installed to serve in the decision making process and to choose the artist and design of the artwork.

By involving the community in the concept development, artist selection, design determination, and then updating them throughout the fabrication and installation process, the public art agency will build its strongest supporters and most vocal advocates. Giving them a place of honor in the dedication ceremony and acknowledging them by name during its proceedings further enhances their trust of the program and willingness to speak out on its behalf in the future.

Section 2: Committees and Coordination

A project's success is defined by more than the completion of the project on time and within budget. In the public art world, 'success' also depends on the degree to which it has fostered a sense of ownership on the part of those that participated in its production. Committees are instrumental in cultivating pride in the finished product and the process by which it came to be. When its dynamics are appropriately aligned, a group of committed and informed individuals representing all project stakeholders can make something truly remarkable happen for its community. This section will describe methods of composing committees that are capable of guiding great art projects to completion, as well as act as effective ambassadors for the public art program's value to the community overall.

Section Topics:
Composition Dynamics
Expertise and Influence
Roles and Expectations
Coordination
Community Engagement

Composition Dynamics:

Size: Committee sizes can vary widely, but as a general rule they should be large enough to represent key skill sets and demographics, while staying small enough to be manageable in terms of scheduling, communications, and coordinating discussion during their actual meetings.

Demeanor: Attitude is an attribute of committee members that often goes ignored until too late. Team players that support the general role that public art plays in making the community a better place to live are obviously preferred. Projects are also best served by those that possess a basic degree of communication skills, and can express their thoughts and opinions in an articulate manner. Consider any known prior relationships between prospective committee members and avoid assembling groups where there may be 'bad blood' between individuals if at all possible.

Expertise and Influence:
In order for the project to be embraced by the community it seeks to serve, specific areas of technical expertise and social influence should be considered when recruiting committee members. Individuals should possess not only the appropriate team-minded demeanor, but be able to provide specific knowledge of the processes of production, design aesthetics, or community networks. The work of public art Selection Committees (SC) are often best served by individuals representing the following fields:

- Architecture
  - Particularly those with experience in public realm projects, such as parks, plazas, and urban design or city planning.
- Visual Arts
  - Practicing Artists
  - Museum Professionals
  - University Studio Art and Art History Professors
  - *Note: It is not advisable to include private gallery representatives on committees due the widespread perception that they will advocate for artists they represent or may have an interest represent in the future.*
- Communities and Neighborhoods
  - Neighborhood Association officers
  - Community Development Corporation staff
  - Civic leaders
- Facility/Site Management
  - Representatives of the building or area where the project is to be installed. For example, if a mural is being painted at a community center, someone from the staff of the community should be included.
- Participating City Bureaus/Departments
  - For example, if the community center were in a city park, then not only would you invite a community center staff person, but a Parks Department representative as well.
- Structural Engineers
  - If sculpture projects of a significant scale are being developed, it is advisable that structural engineers be invited to participate so that someone on the community has the training to ascertain whether or not what the artists propose to build will be structurally sound once installed, and withstand environmental stressors.

Roles and Expectations:
Compose a project-specific orientation brief to acquaint committee members with all the variables of the project beforehand. Factors may include the type of site, preferred artwork type, envisioned scale, budget limit and breakdown, history of the area, the intended use and users of the site, and why the project is being produced in the first place. Send this out beforehand.

Compose a set of project-specific set expectations for committee members including their role, level of decision making authority with an explanation of who else may have 'veto' power (if such a scenario exists), anticipated time commitment, and a provisional schedule of all meetings. Send this along with the orientation brief.

The public art agency staff should be responsible for all correspondence and communication by and between artists applying for percent for art projects and members of selection panels. Discussion by and between any applicant artist and any member of a selection committee outside of regularly scheduled meetings for such purpose during the selection process should be considered grounds for the disqualification of the artist and dismissal of the committee member. Such determination should be made at the sole discretion of the public art agency.

Coordination:

1. Convene the Selection Committee to review the project remit and their expectations, and to discuss the draft of the RFQ or RFP you've sent them to review beforehand. Add relevant comments into the final draft of the document.

2. Distribute the call via the most appropriate means. If the project is a Local-only call, the RFQ/RFP should posted on the public art agency's website, sent to any agency email distribution lists, as well as posted to any official agency social media sites, such as a Facebook page, blog, or a Twitter feed. If the call is Regional or National, it should be posted on the Public Art Network List Serve (administered by Americans for the Arts), as well. Another option for distributing national calls may include posting to Calls for Entry (CaFE). This service requires a fee to post project calls, but their audience of professional artists of high caliber technical expertise and experience producing public art projects is extensive, nationwide.

3. Plan and host any relevant artist information sessions as soon after the RFQ/RFP launch as possible. Many times, artists will have questions about the project that may not be answered in the RFQ/RFP document. This is the public art agency's opportunity address such inquiries.

4. Applications can be submitted in a variety of ways including hard copies through the mail, CD-R's also through the mail, or via digital files. Hard copies pose problems in that while they save the expense of printing off massive amounts of files, they are usually formatted differently from one to another, making it confusing for committee members to interpret. CD-R's likewise pose problems with formatting, as differences in Mac or PC configurations can make files unreadable, plus, they require re-formatting into either a uniform digital format or printing off large amounts of paper. These actions require exorbitant amounts of staff time and expense. Digital submissions are usually more cost-effective, and require less staff time to organize into a coherent form for presentation and discussion.

5. The Committee meets and reviews submissions from artists, including digital images, CV's, and letters of interest. The committee discusses the

submissions and selects up to three finalists to develop a proposal and be interviewed.

6. The Selection Committee reconvenes to interview the finalists about their proposals. This meeting is an opportunity for the Committee to get to know the individual artist's vision, their level of technical expertise, and public art experience, as well as how flexible they are to adaptation and direction from agency staff. Interviews are scheduled 30 minutes apart and usually last 20 minutes each, with 10 minutes for discussion between interviews. At the end of the meeting the committee discusses the interviews and ranks the artists for the project in order of preference. If the project involves artists living outside the local area, telephone and video interviews are also valid.

7. After the finalists are ranked for the project, the public art agency staff will need to call their references. When checking references, it is imperative that they've provided professional contacts that can attest to their working practices, including professionalism, follow-through, capacity for cooperation, and overall degree of organization. Other issues to talk about are how their past projects were received, how the final work is holding up to normal wear and tear, and whether or not their experience working with this artist was a positive one or not. Adaptability, patience, and honesty are also very, very important qualities to learn about. If they have not provided professional contacts from completed projects, demand them. Also, contact representatives from other projects listed on their resume, even if not cited as official references.

8. Once the selected artist is commissioned, agency staff should consider sending the committee members surveys through, gauging the effectiveness of the selection process, and for use in providing testimonials for political advocacy purposes in the annual budget talks with the City Council.

9. Agency staff will need to compose refusal letters for the artists who were not selected, signed by the agency director. These letters should go out as soon as possible after commissioned artist has been selected. In these letters it is often advisable to thank them for their interest, encourage them to apply for future projects, and inform them of the final selection. If hard copy applications or CD-R's were requested, the applicants should have provided self-addressed and stamped envelopes for returning materials.

10. Agency staff should send the first draft of their contract to the selected artist by email first so they can review it. Then, a discussion should be scheduled to cover the payment benchmarks and construction timelines.

11. Once the artist's contract is signed, they should submit a Schematic

Design to the Selection Committee. The Schematic Design consists of general information about what the artist will be performing: conceptual sketch, list of materials, preliminary budget, etc. The committee reviews the Schematic Design to give its feedback, and either approves it or requests changes. The committee should be prepared to continue to meet until the design is satisfactory.

12. Then, the artist submits the Final Design, which includes detailed drawings and other information. The committee reviews the Final Design. The committee must continue to meet until the design is satisfactory. If a stalemate ever occurs in which the committee does not approve the Final Design and the artist refuses to alter the design, it may be necessary to terminate the artist's contract and re-start the project with one of the other finalists that were not originally selected. This should be viewed only as a last resort.

13. Update the committee at the 50% completion mark to keep them engaged and informed.

14. Upon completion of the project, invite members to the dedication ceremony, and acknowledge their participation during the proceedings.

15. Send surveys to committee members to assess the effectiveness of the coordination process for refinement and improvement in future projects.

Community Engagement:
Community members are your most likely and effective allies throughout the project's coordination. You will have made steps to ensure their support by recruiting individual leaders onto the Selection Committee. However, you cannot ensure these individuals will effectively inform their constituents with all relevant information in a timely and consistent manner. Be sure to keep community groups informed about the progress of its development by sending updates to Neighborhood Association leaders, or Community Development Corporation staff (for example) in the form of monthly newsletters or project-specific briefs. As in many cases, photographs speak volumes. Include images of the committee meetings, town hall feedback sessions, artists' information sessions, selected artist's profile and portfolio, final design, etc.

Project Coordination Timeline *(General Guidelines)*

• Confirm site location:	2 months
• Assemble selection committee:	1 month
• Launch RFQ or RFP:	6 weeks - 3 months
• Finalists chosen:	2 weeks
• Artist selected:	1 month
• Artist orientation and contract processed:	1 month
• Schematic Design reviewed:	1 month
• Final Design reviewed:	1 month
• Fabrication:	1-6 months
• Installation:	1 week – 1 month

Section 3: Artist Selection

Methods of artist selection for public art projects vary depending on the size of the budget, the profile of the project, and the complexity of the type of work desired. It is also the most crucial aspect of the entire endeavor. If the 'right' artist is chosen virtually any obstacle can be overcome. Conversely, if the 'wrong' artist is selected for the project, almost nothing will go as planned. In this chapter techniques for thoroughly coordinating the artist selection phase of your public art program will be detailed.

Section Topics:
RFQ/RFP Distribution
Presentation Methods
Committee Reviews
Artist Interviews
Selection Criteria
Artist Contracts/Agreements
Community Engagement

RFQ/RFP Distribution:

Once you've determined whether your project is best suited by issuing either a Request for Qualifications (RFQ) or a Request for Proposals (RFP), you will need to ascertain the most effective means of distributing it so that it garners the attention of as many artists specializing in the type of project you are coordinating as possible. Prior to posting your chosen document on your website, social media outlets, and national listservs, you will need to determine whether your project should only be targeted or reserved to artists living locally, residing regionally, or based in cities nationwide. A number of factors should be considered when making this decision, among them the expertise and skills set required of the project, the project budget, and the envisioned profile of the finished artwork.

Local
Oftentimes, smaller market municipalities are not saturated with artists who've produced large-scale permanent public art installations. In such areas there is usually a lack of educational resources provided in area university art programs for developing the requisite fabrication skills, project management, or business acumen for artists interested in cultivating careers in the public art realm. The result is that local artists may possess excellent foundational skills in terms of composition and design, but lack the first-hand knowledge of how to realize their design concept at a scale appropriate to public art installations. An understanding of the materials and fabrication methods necessary to produce artworks that will perform well over the long term in public settings is likewise most often missing with artists more accustomed to producing work solely for museum or gallery exhibitions. For the most part, RFQ/RFPs should be reserved for local artists alone when the project type is of a medium that requires strong foundational

design and production skills, but less expertise in complex construction methods and project management capacity. Typically, smaller budget projects should be targeted at local issue RFQ/RFP's only. Likewise, if the profile of the project is specifically envisioned for local audiences, then local artists are often the best choice. If your program is interested in developing local expertise, then local-only calls are appropriate also for first-time public artists on small-scale projects with lower budgets as a means of introducing them to the process so that they may learn the system.

Regional

If projects are funded at a larger level, require artists to possess a wider range or more specialized set of fabrication skills, or aims to speak to a broader audience, then it may be appropriate to expand the call-to-artists range beyond a local-only RFQ/RFP. The basic logic is that by extending the geographic radius of eligibility, there will be more artists living within the larger expanse that are likely to be able to produce the project to stakeholders' satisfaction. However, this depends on how large a radius your call allows, and the region's pool of resident artists. Sometimes political concerns may make a regional call an attractive compromise between issuing a local-only and a national-eligibility call. Taxpayers often prefer local artists be given any and all project opportunities funded with public money. However, the fact that local expertise may not fit the skills required of the project make it desirable for the public art agency to recruit regionally. It should be noted on any RFQ/RFP call that local artists are still able to apply to Regional and National calls. Such designations do not exclude local artists, but rather expand the eligibility pool. In the long run, the public is best served by an artwork of high quality, whether produced by a local resident or an artist living outside the region entirely. There is some debate as to whether Regional calls are actually effective in recruiting the highest-level applicant base. Again, this depends on the region. Many suggest that if you are going to expand the eligibility range beyond local that it should be opened up to all artists nationally.

National

If the project's budget is of a size significant enough to warrant artists with demonstrated experience, then a National call is advisable. This increases the likelihood that your applicant pool will contain a number of individuals with proven skills and a portfolio of completed projects over several years that can be assessed for audience reception, maintenance, and project management considerations. Large-scale projects in high profile sites that require complex design principles and construction processes should usually be structured as a National call.

Presentation Methods:

Committee members should be given copies of all applicants' materials prior to the selection meeting in order to structure that session in the most time efficient and process effective manner possible. This may be done in a number of different ways.

1. Paper binders: Compile and collate all artists' materials into a binder for each committee member, with instructions for how to interpret the documents, and a reminder of their expectations as committee members for the specific project. This method is generally the most costly due to printing, binding, and delivery costs, as well as the staff labor that goes into producing each binder. If you choose to present in hard-copy form, it is usually recommended that you require applicants to submit hard copy materials in a standard format. This reduces the cost of printing, and staff time in collating, but requires photocopying and binding, which can get expensive. If you choose this option, you should require all artists to include color copies of their images, and then present committee members color copies for review.

2. Gallery review: Print all artists' materials and post in the public art agency's office in the form of a gallery display around the office walls. Organized alphabetically by artist, this provides committee members an all-in-one opportunity to make ranked preferences in a visual way that many find appealing. The issue with this method is typically access and scheduling. If you can ensure that all committee members can physically visit the office where these materials are displayed within the timeframe indicated for review, then this method can prove very effective.

3. PowerPoints: Delivery of presentations in PowerPoint format is often ideal from the perspective of public art agency staff members due to the ease of use in formatting all applicants' materials into a single document. It saves time in printing, binding, deliver, or posting as a gallery display. However, many times committee members may not have the appropriate technology to access these documents if they are using a computer or software other than that used by the creator of the document.

4. Web-based: Online services such as Basecamp, Google Docs, or Picasa photo albums make for easy uploading of documents and sharing via a hyperlink to invited individuals. These are often the most cost-efficient methods for disseminating large amounts of information to a number of people in the shortest time period. However, technology discrepancies can also pose obstacles to access if committee members do not wish to register with certain programs, or use different operating systems.

5. In-person: Ideally your committee will have been able to review applicant materials before the selection committee meeting. However, this is really most effective only when applicant pools are so large that it would be infeasible for the assembled group to review all materials within the meeting itself. If your pool is small enough, you may consider simply presenting the artists to the committee on the day of the first selection meeting.

NOTE: In the interest of making the most of everyone's time, it is often appropriate for the public art agency staff to remove any applications that do not meet the standards required for the project prior to presenting the most relevant applicants to the committee for consideration. For example, if application materials are formatted poorly or incorrectly, if a national artist applies to a Local-only call, if an artist obviously does not possess the required experience or expertise, or if the quality of work is patently sub-standard, then committee members will most likely appreciate not having to spend their time examining them. Time is a valuable commodity to the public art agency staff and its committee members, and should be focused on delivering the best possible project. Treating sub-standard applications with the same degree of attention that should be devoted to high-quality submissions is not the best use of time, or labor expenses.

Committee Reviews:

Once the method of presentation is decided upon, the following materials should be included for the committee's review.

- **Letter of Interest:** Typed, one-page letter of interest that explains the artist's general concept including theme and materials. They should explain their interest in the project and their general approach to its design and production. Note that this should not take the form of a formal design proposal if responding to an RFQ, but rather a description of their methods for producing a design and finished project if selected. Any proposed designs they choose to submit are entirely optional, and are not compensated unless you've formatted the project call as a RFP.

- **Resume/CV:** Applicants should have submitted their current resume or CV to convey their previous experiences to the selection committee.

- **Images:** Artists submit images of their past and current work. Examples of their work should ideally relate to the project for which they are applying. Each image should be labeled with title, materials, dimensions, site location, commissioning agency, budget, and production duration. Color images are the only type that should be accepted whether you choose to present their materials to the committee in digital or print format.

- **References**: List of three professional references including current phone numbers and/or email addresses. These should be contacts the artist has actually produced work for in the past, ideally public art projects. It is advisable to call each reference to ask of their experience working with the applicant, their project management abilities, budget monitoring diligence, and communication habits, as well as the audience reaction to the finished work of art, and its maintenance needs over time. It is also a good idea to research contacts within organizations for which the applicant may have produced projects listed in their CV, but not cited in the reference list. It is human nature to present their most positive experiences when applying for a commission. However, it is up to you as the public art agency to proactively assess as much of the artists' abilities as possible before hiring them to produce your project. Contacting individuals with whom they may have worked not cited in their reference list may only further support your understanding of them as fully capable. However, it may reveal troubling facts that you need to consider before making final decisions that will affect the project, the public realm, and the future of your public art program.

Selection committee members will ideally have reviewed all submissions prior to the initial selection meeting. At the meeting they view all of the artists' images as a group and discuss issues such as the merits of the artists' work, their previous experience, and the artists' demonstrated skill level with any required materials or production methods stipulated in the RFQ.

If you do not wish to select an applicant outright, the pool should then be narrowed down to a maximum of three (3) finalists who will then go through an interview process with the selection committee. If you choose to request a design proposal from these finalists at this stage, then they should receive an honorarium for the development of an original site-specific design proposal, including budget breakdown. It should be prepared according to specifications appropriate to the project's site context and budget remit. This design proposal should be included as a topic of conversation during the finalist's interview along with other general considerations. Once the final artist is selected, this design will function as their schematic design.

Artist Interviews:

Finalist interviews are ideally always conducted as face-to-face meetings with the selection committee members. Because you may have artists coming in from out of town, scheduling all 3 interviews in the span of a couple of hours is often preferable for committee members. Individual interviews usually last approximately 30 minutes, with 10 minutes between interviewees. When possible, try to schedule the meetings at the project site.

Each artist is asked a series of questions that relate to his or her site-specific proposal as well as their previous work. It is similar to a job interview. Typical questions include:
- o Why are you interested in this project?
- o Have you considered a theme or materials for this project?
- o How do you plan to engage the feedback or participation of the community?
- o How does your current work relate to this project?
- o What is the greatest obstacle you have overcome while working on a project?
- o What experience do you have with managing budgets responsibly?
- o Tell us about any experience that you have had completing major public projects on time and within the budget.
- o What experience do you have coordinating work with engineers, contractors, vendors, and members of the community?

Selection Criteria:

While there are several considerations to take into account when determining the specific project to be installed (see CH1), when selecting the final artist, it primarily comes down to their relevant experience and professional demeanor.

Artists should provide convincing evidence of their ability to successfully complete the project as proposed. Particularly on collaborative or design team projects, artists should demonstrate an ability to:
- Communicate effectively and elicit the ideas of team members;
- Exhibit flexibility and problem-solving skills;
- Work with architectural drawings and construction documents;
- Engage community representatives in a project.
- Successfully manage all aspects of the project including budgets, committees, sub-contractors, installers and other construction and administrative logistics.

In some cases in which budgets are smaller and the project profile is more localized in scale, it may be appropriate to select untested artists new to the field as a means of educating them in the processes of the public art system. However, in these cases, it is advisable that they be directed and coached in their actions by the public art agency staff.

Artist Contracts/Agreements:

Send the first draft of their contract to them by email first so they can review it. If the organization's attorney is not available for responding to all selected artists' questions due to time conflicts, then KPA should designate a single staff person to be the point of contact for any questions regarding artists' questions regarding their contract. This person should be trained how to interpret and explain the document by the organization's legal representative. Any questions requiring a legal opinion should be taken to KPA's Attorney for a decision.

During this time, prepare the project directive and have the organization director and the PKA attorney sign it. After the attorney has returned it to your office, make a copy, and then send the originals to the appropriate authorities within the city administration. The artist should be reviewing their contract during this time BUT NOT SIGNING IT, until the directive is completed and confirmed. Contract signing should not be scheduled or performed until after the city's project directive is completed and confirmed. Work cannot begin until the directive is in place, allowing funds to be dispersed.

Typically, the project manager for the project for which the artist is being commissioned structures the meeting and facilitates discussion on the payment benchmarks schedules to align with construction timelines, but this single staff person designated to explain contracts should be present to finalize contracts with the artists. The organization director must sign the final document.

This session is where you should also discuss the budget structure, making sure they know there is only the amount cited in the RFQ available for this project. By ordinance they are limited to 15-20% of the total budget for their design fee, but they can claim hourly wages from the fabrication budget for their time and labor. The project manager should confirm the budget breakdown with the artist and keep a record on file.

It is important that as project manager you establish the terms of your working relationship with the artist during this session. You want it to be a productive experience for the artist, but it must be made clear that they are working for Public Art Kingsport and the City of Kingsport, not vice versa. The project managers should feel confident that they are responsible for the coordination of the project. Artists must follow their directions, not the other way around.

After the project directive has been signed and returned to your office, three copies of the contract need to be made. The artist should be sent three copies of the contract (for PKA, artist, and City) after the organization director signs them. Two of these contracts need to be returned to your office and then both sent to City signing and one copy returned. After the contract is returned, an invoice can be sent to the City for both the contract signing and the schematic design, which was approved upon the artist's selection. The artist should not begin work until this first check is received. Ideally, it should be processed in 2-3 weeks.

Community Engagement:

While the input of the community is less during the processes of artist selection and contract coordination, they should be notified once a final decision is made and their contracts are completed. Introductory conversations should be scheduled between the artist and any community members that have supported the project's development. Additionally, the artist should also meet with the members of the selection committee once they are commissioned on the project. The selection committee and community representatives can prove to be the most effective ambassadors of the project if they are familiar with the artist's concepts, methods, and vision for the project throughout.

Section 4: Project Management

Projects come to fruition because of the effective coordination of various elements in a professional fashion by your organization's staff. Balancing the demands, schedules, and different working cultures of artists, vendors, government officials, and the general public is both a science and an art. Keeping all stakeholders engaged, committed, and in step throughout the process requires strategic planning and discernment. This section will engage specific processes for guiding the myriad considerations of any project into a coherent and cohesive conclusion that your community can claim with pride.

Section Topics:
Benchmarks: Design, Fabrication, Installation
Invoicing and Payments processing
Vendors, Contractors, and Suppliers
Communication: Artists, Vendors, Contractors, and Committees
Documentation, Promotion, Celebration
Community Engagement

Benchmarks: Design, Fabrication, and Installation

The Project Manager (PM) is the liaison between the artist and the client, the selection committee, the community, the press, the architect, and the general contractor.

The PM should guide the artist through the process by directing their questions to the appropriate people, scheduling committee meetings, helping them connect with the community through meetings or workshops, checking on their fabrication progress, etc.

The selection committee will review the artist's schematic proposal, final design, final installed project, and any changes to the design during the process.

The Project Manager will present the artist's designs to the selection committee, though at times the artist may be asked to do so within the context of a PM coordinated meeting. During the review process, the selection committee may ask for additional information from the artist, or for design changes.

Schematic Designs:
Schematic designs should be as thorough as possible in an effort to streamline the process of payments and production. PM's should provide artists with a set of mandatory items to be produced for the selection committee to consider, detailed in the following table.

Schematic proposal checklist:

Schematic Proposal	Date Due:	Date Reviewed:
Conceptual design – include visuals with specifications about where the artwork will be located at the site.		
Concept statement – narrative account of concept		
Preliminary budget		
Materials – list all materials to be used		
General dimensions		
Approximate weight		
Finish – list the paint and/or coating of the final artwork		
Preliminary maintenance		
Invoice		
Comments:		

Final Design:
Once an artist's schematic design is approved, the final design documents shall include detailed drawings and specifications for materials, site preparation, connections, building interface, and shall also specifically include a detailed colored rendering indicating the exact subject matter and content of the artwork along with the placement of the artwork at the site. The artist should be required to notify their project manager if their final design documents contain any design information that is materially inconsistent with the schematic proposal. The final design documents should also include any other illustrations, renderings, or material details requested by the selection committee or the public art agency staff.

It is imperative that all details of the project are included in the final design. All sizes, materials, colors, attachment methods, budget items, etc., MUST be finalized and presented in these documents. A sample final design checklist is provided below.

Final design checklist:

Final Design		Date Due:	Date Reviewed:
	Detailed drawings/other graphic material (includes color rendering, subject matter/content, and placement of artwork within the site)		
	Materials		
	Site preparation – list any changes necessary to the site		
	Connections – the attachments that will be used to install the artwork		
	Building interface – how will the artwork interact with the building/site		
	Maintenance instructions		
	Revised budget		
	Payment schedule		
	Preliminary installation schedule		
	List of all fabricators and subcontractors, including contact information		
	Invoice		
	Comments:		

The timeframe that artists have to complete their final design varies according to the project timeline established in consultation with the project manager, and approved by the selection committee. However, when drafting artists' contracts it is often useful to include a clause that states that they have up to ninety (90) days to complete and submit final design documents from the date at which their schematic design documents are approved.

On the due date of an artist's final design, the artist should submit all documents listed on the final design checklist to their respective project manager, who will review their submission and confirm that all requested documents are present and completed. The project manager will then present final design documents to the selection committee for review and approval.

The project manager should only submit final design invoices to the client for payment after approval by the selection committee.

Notice to Proceed:
Upon approval of the final design and receipt of payment, the project manager should send the artist a "notice to proceed" letter, stating that fabrication may begin. At that point, the artist should provide:
- Schedule for fabrication and installation that includes a completion date, if one is not already stated as part of a construction project or by the public art agency.
- Description of what elements shall be fabricated by the artist and what elements others shall fabricate.
- List of fabricators, subcontractors and installers that the artist intends to work with, including contact information.
- Payment Schedule, based on anticipated costs for materials, fabrication and installation of the artwork.

Fabrication:
The fabrication must be done in conformity with the approved final design. If the artist has made any changes to the design of the artwork during fabrication, they should notify their project manager before proceeding. Significant changes should be presented to the selection committee for consideration and approval before being permitted to proceed.

The project manager should visit the artist to see the progress of the fabrication. At least one studio visit should be required to approve the 50% completion payment benchmark of the project. The project manager should also call to check on the artist's progress from time to time and address any questions that they may have.

During fabrication, the project manager should also be working with the artist to plan the installation, including coordinating with the project architect and general contractor, as well as coordinating site interface, transportation, scheduling, etc.

Installation, Signage, Post Installation Documentation, Final Payment:
The installation must be scheduled in advance, and must adhere to that schedule. Of course, circumstances beyond one's control should be taken into consideration, but the project manager should be notified if there are any changes to the approved schedule.

Signs identifying the project will need to be provided for in the artist's budget. It is recommended that the public art agency establish a template for project signage language and materials, then require artists to use the same vendor in order to ensure uniform quality.

After the installation is finished, the artist should notify their project manager in writing that it is complete. With this letter, the artist should include a CD of digital images as a means post installation documentation, along with written maintenance instructions, and their final invoice.

Artwork Dedication Event:
To celebrate the completion of a project, the project manager should work with the artist and all relevant stakeholders to plan an artwork dedication event. Such events should ideally be scheduled at a time when the most members of the surrounding community are available to attend, and then coordinated with the calendars of those relevant political authorities whose support was important to the project's success. During the proceedings, the artist should be given their credit and allowed to say a few words of thanks. Members of the selection committee, city department officials, and community stakeholders should also be acknowledged. If the mayor or city council representative for the district in which the project is located are available to make remarks, it is greatly advisable that they be given the opportunity to do so.

Timeline worksheet:

X	Tasks (SAMPLE)	Estimated Completion	Actual Completion
	Contract signed		
	Invoice for signing of contract		
	Schematic proposal due		
	Schematic proposal review		
	Schematic proposal changes due (if applicable)		
	Schematic proposal approved		
	Invoice for schematic proposal		
	Community involvement (if applicable)		
	Final design due		
	Final design review		
	Final design changes due (if applicable)		
	Final design approved		
	Invoice for final design		
	Notification to commence fabrication		
	Fabrication commenced		
	50% completion		
	Fabrication completed		
	Installation commenced		
	Installation completed		
	Post-installation documentation and maintenance requirements received		
	Final acceptance – approved by selection committee		
	Notification of final acceptance		
	Invoice for final acceptance		
	Dedication Ceremony (if applicable)		

Invoicing and Payments processing:

Ideally, artists should receive payment within 3 days of the public art agency receiving payment from the client. Payment turnaround varies per client, but it is common for processing times to range from 21 days to over 90 days when working on municipally funded projects. It is best to thoroughly discuss all payment needs with the artist prior to the contract signing and align payment benchmarks in such a manner that they are able to purchase materials and maintain steady production progress in the event that any delays in invoice turnaround occurs.

Many government-funded projects require completion of work in full before payment will be dispersed. This model is not possible with most artists working on public art projects. Most are not incorporated, and do not have business credit lines available to them to the extent that would allow purchase of materials and payment of outside contractors on the front end of the project.

Because of the prolonged timeline required by requisite committee approvals and invoice processing protocols, artist payments should be structured in allotments triggered by the fulfillment of specific project design and fabrication benchmarks. The smoother their benchmark approvals are granted by the selection committee, the faster invoices can be submitted. The swifter invoices can be processed, the timelier the project can be completed. Without the consistent flow of resources, the project will be subject to the possibility of prolonged delays.

Artists must often coordinate several projects simultaneously in order to make a living. If your project is held up by prolonged payment delays, they will have no choice but to direct their attention to other projects that provide payments more reliably. By the time your project's payment is processed, the artist may be in the middle of finishing up work on other projects, which means yours may have to wait even longer for fabrication to resume.

Producing a finished work for reimbursement on the back end after fabrication and installation are totally finished is simply not an option for public art unless the agency is purchasing previously made works for installations or displays that are not site-specific commissions. Examples of this sort would include the agency buying paintings and drawings available from artists' studios to display in municipal office buildings, community centers, schools, and libraries, etc.

Vendors, Contractors, and Suppliers:

When artists state their preferred vendors, contractors, and suppliers, for providing services on a public art project, it is highly recommended that they be thoroughly researched. Likewise, before making any recommendations to artists for outside service or materials providers, all such contractors should be vetted prior to such suggestion of a pairing. Researching contractors through entities such as the Better Business Bureau, the Chamber of Commerce, or Dunn and Bradstreet can provide confidence that your project's partners are sound and reliable. If discrepancies are found that raise concern that transactions shall proceed in an orderly fashion, then it is an opportunity to consult with the artist to source another supplier or service provider.

In terms of payments to vendors, unless the public art agency is willing to assume liability, it should made clear to the artist that they will be solely responsible for ordering and paying for all materials, supplies, and outside labor. Some artists mistakenly assume that they can simply provide a materials list to the public art agency for fulfillment. This can put the public art agency at risk of litigation if payment is not forthcoming within vendors' time constraints. The artist is the contracted entity that is commissioned to coordinate all materials, supplies, and labor transactions related to the completion of the project.

Communication with Artists, Vendors, Contractors, and Committees:

Communication between all parties involved in the project's completion is a vital component to the timely coordination of its various activities. The ideal scenario is one in which the project manager is the conduit of all communication from all project stakeholders. It is crucial that all parties involved understand this protocol. If artists are talking to committee members, or community groups are in dialogue with committee members or artists without the knowledge of the project manager, the cogency and completeness of information required to complete the project is diffused with every instance. Such casual conversations can easily lead to decisions on the part of some to try to change the results of official meetings, subverting the integrity of the process, and diminishing the perceived legitimacy of the public art agency as the coordinating authority. Project managers should establish this protocol with all stakeholders at the very beginning of the planning process. The public art agency is the leader and its directives must be followed.

Methods of communication are important to consider as well. In the case of artists, and those with whom the project manager will need to have frequent contact, email and telephone are preferable. Official notices regarding contracts, project benchmarks, and invoices should always be issued in hard-copy form, as well as digitally, as a back-up measure. Project managers should always be proactive in their contact with all project correspondence, never assuming that since an email was sent or a voicemail left, that it is the responsibility of the other party to return contact in a timely manner. Keeping a communications log for each project is often helpful in moving project business forward.

Some web-based project management platforms offer the ability to stage teleconferencing with multiple parties while all can view design documents and photos. Others offer video-conferencing with similar capabilities. Take advantage of such services to minimize scheduling logistics, and saving time for stakeholders. The easier the project manager can make participation, the more likely it is that all parties involved will want to engage in the project's successful outcome. Something to mindful of, however, is opening up the discussion remotely via group email or group commenting on web-based documents. Without the leadership and guidance of the project manager to explain documents and answer questions, comments can quickly express misinterpretations of the material and cause confusion and apprehension. Discussion of project documents need to be coordinated by the project manager in real time, not via email. This is especially important in regards to design documents.

Documentation, Promotion, Celebration:

The project manager should be conscientious about documenting key points of the project's development throughout its coordination. From the first meeting of the selection committee, the artist's orientation, design review meetings, community development gatherings, fabrication processes, and project installations, photographs should tell the story of a project's coming to life. The artist should also be providing photos of fabrication and installation, as well as copies of their design documents. Budget worksheets and benchmark checklists should also be retained the project's work file by the project manager. Hard copies should be scanned and saved digitally as a back up to paper copies.

Dedication ceremonies are also an excellent promotional opportunity for the public art agency. Retain a designated photographer to document the occasion. Instruct them to take photos of the artist next to the work, alongside members of the community, selection committee, and political authorities. It is also beneficial for future advocacy and funding to show members of the public art agency staff in these shots. These images can be used on the agency website, publications, press kits, and annual reports in the future.

Contact the local print media prior to the event with a press release providing all the pertinent details of the project, its artist, subject matter, process of community support, etc. Matters of budget and funding should be given only if specifically requested, and then only in precise terms in which its breakdown is made clear. It is often advisable when discussing budgetary matters of public art projects to explain how funds are allocated, that a certain percentage went to the artist for design, a different percentage for fabrication by outside contractors, a percentage for materials, and supplies, etc. Stressing the local economic impact of a project's funding is also wise. Emphasizing the dollars that were paid to local vendors, suppliers, and contractors for goods and services, for example, is important in making the general public understand that public art projects are in essence construction projects with a direct impact on the local economy.

Community Engagement:

During this phase of the project, the surrounding neighborhood should be kept apprised of the progress with photos and brief bulletins. This is often most effectively communicated in the form of an email newsletter, although in some cases in which access to technology is limited, it may be necessary to visit community association meetings with hard-copy bulletins including photos and relevant details. It is important to sustain the support of the local community throughout the project, and regular updates are a vital part of this endeavor.

One means of building community support and excitement for the project during its fabrication is to stage a visit to the artist's studio or contractor's fabrication facility, if the work is produced locally. An artist's talk about the project's concepts, design, and processes of production are often compelling insights for the general public unfamiliar with how public artworks are made. Sharing the behind the scenes details with the community is often a great way to enable its members to contribute to the project's ultimate success by sharing its story inflected with these types of personal experiences. Garner testimonials and feedback from community members during such occasions for inclusion in annual reports and promotional material for the public art agency's work in future advocacy and fundraising initiatives.

Chapter 5: Inventory and Maintenance

As a city's public art collection grows, it is imperative that its art works be maintained in a manner appropriate to the materials and installation setting of each piece. A major consideration is how routine conservation and major repairs are funded once a project's primary budget is fully spent. This section will cover issues to do with record keeping for completed projects, appropriate conservation methods, and financing options for ensuring budgets for maintenance are sustainable.

Section Topics:
Cataloguing
Cleaning
Repairs
Budgets
Community Engagement

Cataloguing:
An accurate and accessible archive is a tremendous resource for any public art agency. Not only can it be a source of relevant project data for formatting reports, or performing maintenance, but it can also be a tool for developing advocacy initiatives and cultivating stakeholders for the public art program overall. Some simple steps should be taken into account when building such a database.

A standard format for labeling all documents should be adopted in order to ease the process of locating information in computer shared files. Without a standardized labeling system, documents can easily be misfiled and time is swiftly wasted in compiling relevant information. Clear instructions on what types of documents to file under what category should be distributed to the office staff using the same shared folders as well. By decreasing time spent on mundane administrative tasks such as searching for files, the productivity of the staff can be improved as a whole. A model for labeling would be to abbreviate the public art agency's name to its initials, then the project name, the year, and the artist's name. An example label would then read:

Organization Name-ArtWalk-Date-Artist Name.doc

Photograph formats vary widely, but for most purposes JPEG is the most usable. File sizes make a difference, with higher resolution being best for presentations where images are to be projected on a large scale. If images are to be used for printed pieces, the printer may request an image size of 300dpi or more. In order to ensure your photos are versatile, be sure to take high-resolution photos of key events, and of installed artwork, and label them as such.

Various online services are available for storing photographs, which makes sharing large format images and files easier than emailing or shipping a CD-R.

While Basecamp and other platforms that offer conference calling and business management capabilities charge a monthly fee, there are free tools such as Picasa through Google which allows up to 1,000 images in a single album with captioning that can be shared with others via an invitation link. This tool can also be useful when conducting committee review meetings.

As a matter of contingency planning it is advisable to assemble all project materials into a hard-copy file in the form of a project binder. All documents related to the project should be kept in the binder, including the minutes of all selection committee meetings, the RFQ copy, the selected artist's initial submission materials, schematic and final designs, photographs, copies of receipts, and transcripts of project-related correspondence (especially email).

Cleaning:
While most public art pieces in the exterior built environment may never require cleaning of any kind due to their material composition and method of construction, occasional cleaning will enhance their impact within the community and is recommended on an as-needed basis. For example, metal sculptures fabricated from stainless steel and aluminum, etc., will often see a build up of grime due to exposure to the elements. This is usually remedied with a gentle dish soap and water solution, applied as a spray then washed away with a soft fabric cloth. Harsh chemical solvents are not recommended, as certain industrial grade cleaners contain ingredients that may corrode sealants or paints applied to metal surfaces, and even damage the metal itself. Certain metals will naturally acquire a patina over time such as bronze and copper, which take on a greenish hue, or core-ten steel, which oxidizes in the open air as a means of protecting the metal itself. These phenomena are traditionally not redressed by cleaning, but are rather left alone.

Exterior mural paintings will weather over time, and may require a gentle wash down on an as-needed basis with water.

Interior pieces will require a regular dusting to ensure they retain a mint appearance, but rarely much more.

An audit of the public art collection should be scheduled at regular intervals to ascertain any cleaning needs.

Repairs:

Unless notified that a public art piece is in need of repair, plan on examining all pieces for any conservation or restoration needs during the audit for cleaning. The first choice for making repairs should be the artist that produced the piece in the first place. If the artist that made the work is not available or able to perform repairs, then any major repairs should be performed by experienced professionals that are accustomed to working with the materials of its construction.

Budgets:
Maintenance is often a neglected consideration when planning projects, to the detriment of the community, and the reputation of the public art agency. There are various means by which to allocate funds for upkeep and repairs. One method is to retain a percentage of the overall project budget for maintenance of each specific artwork. Another is to establish a separate funding line within the public art agency's annual budget that is designated solely for maintenance purposes of the entire public art collection, as needed. For the most part, annual maintenance costs tend to be very low because public art projects are subject to such scrutiny throughout their design, fabrication, and installation phases, that the end result can normally be expected to last several years without the need for little more than routine cleaning. If the public art agency has been diligent with inspecting the work of their commissioned artists, the public should expect finished projects that are 'built to last.' The real necessity for maintenance funds comes not from routine cleaning, however, but when disaster strikes in the form of vandalism, accidental damage, or a catastrophic weather event. If such instances occur, then costs can be high in order to restore the piece to its previous condition. Without dedicated funds in place to address these unexpected acts, outside resources will need to be garnered in the form of private donations or in-kind support in the form of materials, supplies, and volunteer labor.

Community Engagement:
The role of the community in assisting with ongoing maintenance is a vital one. Area residents will be the most immediate and consistent source of information regarding the condition of the artwork year round. Communities with which the public art agency has built strong ties of participation in the project's development and success have a tendency to feel a greater sense of ownership with the piece, and will often discourage acts of vandalism. If the artwork is damaged, or requires routine maintenance, it is most often the residents of the community that report its condition. Consider hosting a community clean-up day every other year as a means of sustaining ties to the neighborhood in which projects are installed. These events can be enlivened with music, refreshments, and games to create memorable experiences that bond members of the community more closely with the work of art, as well as the public art agency, and with each other.

www.ingramcontent.com/pod-product-compliance
Lightning Source LLC
Chambersburg PA
CBHW070743180526
45168CB00004B/1514

* 9 7 8 1 5 0 8 9 6 4 5 7 5 *